Chronological History of the Mosher Family

Genealogical Records and Anecdotes of the Moshers, from the 1700s to 1891

By William Mosher

PANTIANOS
CLASSICS

Published by Pantianos Classics

ISBN-13: 978-1-78987-337-5

First published in 1891

Contents

Chronological Data Respecting the Mosher Family

The following data with reference to the Mosher Family, of which there are many connections in the county of Hants and other counties of the Province and Canada, will be read with interest. They have been carefully compiled by William Mosher, of Mosherville, Hants, after considerable research and trouble.

Ezeziel Mosher, the Ancestor of the Mosher Family in the United States and Canada

Ezekiel Mosher lived in Manchester, England, according to the records, in the 17th century. Hugh Mosher, his son, came to Rhode Island with Lydia Maxon, his wife, in the 17th century; also, Daniel and family, and John, a bachelor, sons of the above Ezekiel. Daniel and family and John were massacred by Indians. The old man Ezekiel came out to Rhode Island soon after his sons, and died, leaving Hugh his only heir; Hugh having one daughter and five sons, their names as follows: — Rebecca, John, James, Nicholas, Joseph and Daniel. Hugh, the son of Ezekiel, he being the second generation from Ezekiel, died in 1713.

The Third Generation

Nicholas, of Hugh, had ten children, their names being as follows: — Hugh, born November 16th, 1690; Joseph, born April 7th, 1692; Mercy, born December 16th, 1695; Elizabeth, born April 16th, 1697; Thomas, born February 26th, 1699; Nicholas, born January 1st, 1702; Mercy, born July 6th, 1705; Rebecca, born March 20th, 1707; Ephraim, born March 5th, 1709; Margaret, born January 17th, 1712. As will be seen there were two Mercys in the family; the eldest died before the last was born. Joseph, son of Hugh, had eight children: — Rebecca, born December 28th, 1695; Philip, Jonathan, Joseph, James, Ruth, Benjamin and William, the latter the youngest, born July 24th, 1713.

The Fourth Generation

Nicholas, of Nicholas, grandson of Hugh, had the following children: Freelove, Margaret, Mercy, Elizabeth, Susannah, James, Nicholas, Wilcox, Jabez, Rebecca and Deliverance.

The Fifth Generation

James Mosher, son of the above Nicholas, married Lydia Allen and had the following children: — Olive, who married Capt. Jehu Rowland, in 1780, and did not come to

Nova Scotia with the rest of the family. She died in Washington County, N. Y., March 19th, 1837. James and Lydia and some three or four of the children who were born at the date of their departure, 1760, came to Nova Scotia and landed at a creek on the Avon River, with several others from Rhode Island, and named the place Newport Landing. The Post Office at that place is still called Newport Landing, and the place re-named Avondale by the late inhabitants. James Mosher was one of the seventy proprietors who took up the Township of Newport, which comprised some twelve miles square, more or less. The family of the said James Mosher and Lydia comprised Amy, Sarah, Jehu, Barzillai, Lydia, Allen, Deliverance, Rhoda, Nicholas, Joseph, George and Elizabeth; the first four were born in Rhode Island, the remainder in the Township of Newport. James Mosher was a millwright, and built the first mill in the Township of Newport for grinding grain for the seventy proprietors, which was built where Alexander Cochran now has mills on the River Herbert. The mill was to be finished in October, 1761, but some accident happened and it was not finished until the fall of 1762. John Chambers was to attend the mill, and the agreement was to take a pint less out of the grain per bushel than the inhabitants outside of the Township, Also the proprietors were to be accommodated first, viz., two coming together, the proprietor would get his grist first.

Thomas Allen, a brother of Mrs. James Mosher, came from Rhode Island when James and family emigrated to

Nova Scotia. He was one of the seventy proprietors of the Township of Newport; also John Anthony, who married Ruth Allen, a sister of Mrs. James Mosher, but who was not one of the proprietors. He settled in Douglas, on the Kennetcook River, the first farm east of the Township line, and bounding on said line of Township between Newport and Douglas. Their family comprised Noah, Alice, Annie, James, David, and John. They left other children in Rhode Island. Noah Anthony married Agnes Harvie, a daughter of Amy Mosher and Archibald Harvie. Alice Anthony married Ezekiel Marsters; Annie Anthony married John Burgess, and lived on north side of Kennetcook River, near the mouth, now called Burlington. John Anthony and Ruth died and were buried on the farm, now called the Anthony burying-ground, where many of their friends lie to-day, 1891.

The Sixth Generation

Amy Mosher, of James and Lydia, married Archibald Harvie, and had John, Robert, Nicholas, Archibald, Barzillai, Agnes and Lydia. The last named married Archibald Harvie, who was blind of one eye, and went by the name of blind Arch.

Sarah Mosher, of James and Lydia, married James Campbell, and had the following: — Gazelda, Archibald, Colin, Malcolm, John, Daniel, Dougall, Mary, Amy, Sarah, Lydia, Lucy, and Hannah.

Jehu Mosher, of James and Lydia, married Hannah Greeno, and had Olive, Sarah, Lydia, Jehu, Daniel, James, Nicholas, Allen, Reuben, Matilda, Priscilla, and Hannah. In a short time Hannah Greeno died, and Jehu married Eleanor Foley, and she had Noah, Ark, Branch, Rachel, Nelson, Sarah Freelove, William, Martha, George H., and Wesley. Jehu had a farm near where his father landed, and was quite a business man, and was very strong. It is said of him that he carried an anchor for a wager that weighed nearly 500 pounds, thirty feet on a wharf. It was raised to his shoulder, and he walked the thirty feet. Said he did not breathe while the anchor was on his shoulder, and his feet burst out through his thin shoes, which were new. This was all the harm done. He gained the bet, and lived until he was 97 years old.

Barzillai Mosher, of James and Lydia, married Margaret Harvie, and had Barzillai, James, Archibald, Nicholas, Lydia, Joseph, Amy, John, Agnes, and Margaret. The above Barzillai (of Barzillai) was a sea-captain. He was lost at sea, and nothing was ever heard of him or any of the crew. John was also a sea-captain, and died in Windsor, N.S.

Lydia Mosher, of James and Lydia, married John Densmore, of Noel, Hants Co., the offspring being John, James, Frank, Mary, Samuel, Nicholas, Jenny, Olive, Letitia, Lydia, and Amy. Jenny married John Anthony, of the above John Anthony; Olive married Nicholas Harvie, son of the above Archibald and Amy; Letitia married Samuel Densmore, known as Deacon Sam; Mary married Robert

Greeno; Lydia married John Densmore, at the head of the Marsh; Amy married Samuel Densmore, known as Sleepy Sam.

Allen Mosher, of James and Lydia, married Esther Wilcox, of Kempt. He had a large piece of land, and settled down to farming. They had the following children: — Jehu, Robert, Wilcox, Fanny, Polly, Simon, Amy, Benjamin, Rebecca, Allen, and Lydia, and three died young. Total, 14. The above went by the name of the Kempt Moshers.

Nicholas Mosher, of James and Lydia, married Polly Greeno, who was a daughter of Daniel Greeno, who came from Rhode Island with his brother Moses. Nicholas and Polly had fifteen children — Jehu, Rachel, Mary, James, Amy, Abigail, Lydia, Olive, Nicholas, Tonge, George, Daniel, John A., Elizabeth and Sarah.

Joseph Mosher, of Jas. and Lydia, married Priscilla Greeno, and had the following children: James, Barzillai, Daniel, Elizabeth, Nicholas, Joseph, Mary, William, Amy and George.

George Mosher, of James and Lydia, (he being of the sixth generation), married Margaret Thompson and had the following children: — William, Lydia, Cyrus, Eliza, Darius, Ira, Nicholas, James and Margaret.

Deliverance Mosher, of James and Lydia, married John Macumber, their family being as follows: — Ichabod, Nicholas, Girden, Stephen, Jehu M., Michael, Deliverance, Lydia, Susannah and Sarah.

Rhoda Mosher, of James and Lydia, married Simon Ward, and had the following children: — James, Robert,

Increase, Sarah, Mary, Martha, John, Margaret, Lucy and Susannah.

Elizabeth Mosher, of James and Lydia, married James Constantine. They had six of a family: — Pharoz, William, James, Catherine, Elizabeth and Rhoda.

The above Nicholas and Polly lived on a farm owned by their Father James, bounded East by the Township line between Newport and Douglas, North by the Kennetcook River, over a mile from Township line west, thence Southerly to base line, so called, over a mile, thence to Township line, making over a mile square, and a river running from Rawdon down through centre of farm, emptying into the Kennetcook River. The said Nicholas was a carpenter and a very persevering mechanic. He took a contract to build a vessel, which was constructed a quarter of a mile up from the mouth of the little river, and was superintended by John Corney, and launched into said river about 1807. Was sloop-rigged, carried a square topsail, and was sailed for a time by a stranger, afterward by Captain Barzillai Mosher (of the above Barzillai), of the sixth generation. This vessel carried plaster from Newport to Philadelphia, with a capacity of about 60 tons. After a time was sold. She was the first vessel built in Newport, Hants County, N.S.

The above farm was willed to Nicholas and Joseph Mosher, sons of James. They died, and were buried a few rods from the little river opposite where the sloop was built, with others. The farm was sold to strangers, not any of the name living on it now, (but nearby). Joseph Mosher, of James, was a carpenter and hewer of timber. He used a broad-axe eleven inches wide on the bit, and weighed eleven pounds. I am told that some men in that day used axes weighing thirteen pounds. Joseph and family lived on the farm willed to Nicholas and Joseph. There were two old houses on it, but very little land cleared, and Joseph got tired of hewing and working around by the day to maintain a family; and as he concluded that the farm was not large enough for two large families, he went up to the head of Kennetcook River, took up land and chopped a field (it being all woods), built a house out of round logs, and covered the roof with spruce bark, gathered moss and caulked the cracks between the logs, and moved his family in. Burnt off the chopping, cleared out the stuff remaining and burnt it; then sowed wheat and barley; had no team, covered the grain with a hack. This hack was made like a three-tined fork, with about four inches of the tines turned down so as to form a three-toothed rake, with which he raked the ground so as to cover the grain; and planted potatoes dropped on the ground two and a half feet apart, and with a hoe called a grub hoe hoed the ground up on to the potatoes, covering a certain depth. This formed the hill. Then after potatoes came up hoed dirt around again, and by this means raised a great crop of potatoes.

After he got the grain gathered and threshed a trouble came to him to get it ground, as there was no mill nearer than eight miles through the woods to Noel, and only a path blazed out, and no road. The way he got the grain to mill was to get about one and a half bushels in two bags, making three bushels in all; put one bag on his shoulder and carried about half a mile, then laid it on a stump and went back for the other bag, carried it a half mile past where he left the first, hung it on a tree, and called it resting while he walked back to where he had left the other bag. Then took that on his shoulder and carried past the other bag half a mile, and hung it up, and repeated the process until he reached the mill. Now the readers will see the distance travelled to get the flour home, carrying flour the same way; but in winter he had a toboggan, and if snow was deep, weald put on snowshoes, and draw quite a grist to mill. The barley he hulled in a mortar, with which soup was made. The mortar he made by taking a hardwood log three feet long and eighteen inches over, hacked and cut with such tools as he had at the end, then made a fire of short, dry wood in the hole, keeping a wet cloth around the edge while burning it; then chiselled and cut, then burned, and so on, until he got a hole twelve inches over and fifteen inches or more deep, and scraped clean. The mortar was then complete. The lower end of the pestle was made to fit the bottom of the mortar, and a hole bored through it, say, eighteen inches from lower end, into which a long handle was fitted to use with both hands. He would then get up on a block, put some barley in the mortar, and pound away until he got the hulls separated from the barley. This he would do in the evening, and next day would have a nice dish of barley soup.

As soon as the neighbours heard of the mortar, they would get a little bag of barley and go over to Uncle Joe's (as they called him) in the evening, and they would pound out their grist and have a pot of soup next day. In this way he got a job of making several mortars. Neighbours were scarce. A Mr. Ryan and a Mr. Lahey lived, with their families, on the next farms each way from him. Mr. Ryan had a daughter Jenny, and Daniel Mosher, of Joseph, married her. Mr. Lahey had a daughter Rachel, and she married and had a daughter Harriet, who is the wife of the writer. All went well for a time. The older boys helped to farm and worked out, some to get clothes and shoes, and save provision at home. Joseph himself hired out at times for neighbours and friends. All did the best they could, until Priscilla (Joe's wife) got sick. There was no doctor nearer than Newport, no ploughed road, and no waggon to drive, if they could. So they concluded to make a machine like a bier. The poles were long and tapered at the ends, so as to go into a stirrup of a saddle; boards were nailed across the centre of the poles, and a box made on it to admit of a bed. The sick woman was put in the bed, the handles placed through the stirrups of forward horse, the other end through the stirrups of the hind horse's saddle, and a man on each saddle to guide the horses and steady the bed. Elizabeth rode behind the last man to wait on her mother, and in this way she was carried down to the house she had moved from. The distance was about twenty-three miles, but the mother was so far gone with consumption, that the doctor could do nothing for her, and she died April 17th, 1813. Joseph broke up housekeeping after she died. The children got scattered. George, the youngest, was only a little over five years old. The old mill in Noel failed to grind, and Mr. Densmore had it removed and commenced to erect a new mill in the fall.

Jehu Mosher, of Nicholas, was the millwright. The writer's father went with him to serve his time before his mother died. They got the mill well under way, and they agreed with a man at Mount Denson, in Township of Falmouth, to make the stones, there being no stone of the right grit nearer, and he was to deliver at Mitchener's point, at the mouth of Avon River, on the beach, a little below high-water. He did so, and left the stones standing on edge with a pole run through the eyes of the stones, so a boat could come and get them. John Densmore was to send for them; but, it being late, cold weather set in, the ice made around the stones and pole so great a cake, that in March a southerly storm and high tide came which lifted the cake of ice and stones, and the wind drove them out into Minas Basin. Then wind and tide shifted, and drove the field of ice up the Bay, and forced the ice and stones into Noel Bay, and ashore in the mouth of Noel River, and there remained until the April sun thawed away the ice from the stones. Some party being out to see if there was a chance to get the boat off to go for the stones, to his great surprise saw the stones standing on edge, with the pole through the eyes, as they were left off Mitchener's Point, not one and a half miles from the mill. They were soon hauled to the mill and put in place. The old women concluded the Lord knew they had been suffering for bread all winter, and had sent the stones in this mysterious manner fully one month before they could have got them in any other way, being fifty miles by land and thirty by water from Mitchener's Point, and dare not risk an open boat across the Bay before the last of April.

Then, when the mill was ready, — Joseph Mosher had given up housekeeping, and their children scattered, — they concluded to send for him, (as he was a miller), and he went and got the mill to work. The women concluded that was a God-send to have a good miller, and the barley mortar was set aside in Noel, and at the head of Kennetcook River, as people there had to carry the grain in the same way as Joseph did, but hulled it in the mill. They also rejoiced with their Noel friends and vicinity, and for a long time talked of Providence sending the stones in such a mysterious manner, and also of getting the miller. He taught the son John the trade of grinding, and after the old man, Joseph, came away, John went by the name of miller John Densmore, as long as he lived, there being other Johns. Joseph came to Newport, lived with his son Barzillai a while, then with his son James for a time, then came and lived with his son Joseph. After a few years he took the bowel or summer complaint, and only lived three days. He had always enjoyed good health. He died August 19th, 1859, aged 90 years, 10 months and 5 days.

The above narrative I write to let the young generations know of the hardships their ancestors had to endure in the settling of this new country.

The Seventh Generation

Jehu Mosher, of Jehu, married Mary Burgess, and had the following children: — Silas, Sarah, John Edward, Ann, Hannah Jane, Matilda, Jehu Allen, and Ezekiel.

Daniel Mosher, of Jehu, married Levina Black, and had the following children:— Hannah, Jehu, Eliza, Matilda, Reuben, Archibald, Barzillai, Sarah, and William. Daniel and family moved to Ontario, and the two latter children were born in that province.

James Mosher, of Jehu, married Mary Smith, (of Thomas and Lydia Smith), their family consisting of lamina, Matilda, Daniel, Thomas Harding, Lydia Ann, James Allen, Mary Letitia, Calvin Smith, and Sarah Eliza. The above James Mosher was a shoemaker and tanner of leather, who resided in Newport for a time, and then moved to Chester, N.S. He did an extensive tanning business in Chester, and stood high in society. Was a prominent member of the Baptist Church, and finally closed up the business and came back to Windsor, where he died.

Nicholas Mosher, of Jehu, married Nancy Malcom, their offspring being: — James, Melinda, Sarah Jane, Nicholas, Elizabeth, Margaret M., Hannah, Matilda, and Daniel. The above Nicholas was a ship-builder, and was a member of the Provincial Parliament for the County of Hants, N.S., for a number of years.

Allen Mosher, of Jehu, married Jenny Proctor, and had five children, — James Taylor, William, John Allen, Olive, and Melinda Jane. The above John Allen Mosher is in the Methodist ministry.

Reuben Mosher, of Jehu, married Elizabeth Mosher, of Joseph, their children being, — Reuben, Priscilla, Daniel, Joseph, Thomas, James, George, and Hannah.

Matilda Mosher, of Jehu, married Geo. Armstrong, of Kempt, Hants Co., and had the following children: — George, Thomas, Jane, Priscilla, Fish, Daniel, Joseph, Elias, and Hannah.

Priscilla Mosher, of Jehu, married George Malcom, and had the following: — Matilda, Hannah Jane, Allen, John, and Fanny.

Hannah Mosher, of Jehu, married George Fox, and had seven of a family, — Levina, Sarah, Judson, John, Melinda, Lydia, and Thomas.

Noah Mosher, of Jehu, married Eliza Stillman, and had the following children: — Rachel Salome, Omen Edward, Clementina, Amanda, Noah, Damarius, and Leander.

Rachel Dove Mosher, of Jehu, married Peleg Sanford, and had the following children: — James Hiram, Charles Wesley, William Wilson, George Nelson, Fred. Curry, Sarah Ellen, and Delphina.

Branch Mosher, of Jehu, married Sophia Lockhart, and had one child named James Branch Mosher. Sophia died, and Branch married Sophia's sister, who had one child. They both died, and Branch also.

James Branch Mosher, of B., married the widow Morris, she having no issue by James B. He was a fine mechanic, a ship-joiner, and did the work of joining of many ships at Avondale. When his health failed, he moved to Water-town, Mass., in 1888, and is now doing some light work in a factory and making a comfortable living.

Sarah Freelove Mosher, of Jehu, married William Chambers, and had the following offspring: — Loran, Angelina, Collonwood, Seymour, Henrietta, and Arthur.

Nelson Mosher, of Jehu, married Margaret Murphy, of Capt. Thomas, and had the following family: — Annet, Narraway, Ellen, and Margaret. Margaret died, and Nel-son, after a time, married Margaret's sister Catharine, the children by this second marriage being, — Almona, Lilly, and McKewen. Nelson was a sea-captain. He came home sick, and died, after severe sufferings.

William Mosher, of Jehu, married Maria Harvie, of Woodbury, and had the following: — William Peoples, Wilson, and Woodbury. After Maria died, William married Mary Bell, of St. John, N.B., and had the following family: — Nelson, Norman, and Charles. William was a seaman, and was washed overboard from the barque "Eugena," and drowned.

Martha Mosher, of Jehu, married Capt. James W. An-thony, of Jacob, and had the following children: — Napo-leon, Leila, Rachel, Vincent, Wesley, Alfonso, Clarence, and Leberta. When Leberta was young, not quite in her teens, Capt. A. died of heart disease in Antwerp, when quite a young man.

George H. Mosher, of Jehu, married Mary Warnock, and had the following children: — Ovilla. Major, Orilla, Clementine, and Georgia.

Wesley Mosher, of Jehu, married Betsy Maddox, of Bridgeport, Conn., U.S., and had the following: — Eleanor, Arthur, Frederick, and Leila. Wesley is in the employ of Wheeler and Wilson, in the sewing-machine business, making the eyes in needles for the last twenty-five years.

Barzillai Mosher, of Barzillai, never married. He was drowned at sea. He is said to have been a fine sea-captain. He sailed a sloop built at what is now called Mosherville, Hants Co., Nova Scotia.

James Mosher, of Barzillai, married Susannah Black, and had the following children: — Alexander, Barzillai, Philip, John, Sarah, Margaret, Mary Ann, and Amy.

Archibald Mosher, of Barzillai, never married. He died in Newport when well advanced in years.

Nicholas Mosher, of Barzillai, married Abigail Bailey, and died without issue.

Lydia Mosher, of Barzillai, married John Forrest, their issue being as follows: — Barzillai, Ezra, Harkanus, John, Joseph, George, and James.

Joseph Mosher, of Barzillai, married Hannah Fish. They had one girl, who died without a name, and another daughter named Lydia, who died at the age of i8 years. Her mother died soon after the last child was born, and Joseph, several years after, was drowned in the St. Croix River, near his home.

Amy Mosher, of Barzillai, married Alexander Miller, and had the following children: — William Alexander and John Barzillai, twins; also Martha and Agnes.

John Mosher, of Barzillai, married the widow McKenzie, formerly Mary Ward, and had the following children: — Adelaide and Adeline, they being twins.

Agnes Mosher, of Barzillai, married Philip Smith, and had the following children: — Margaret Ann, Thomas Israel, Alexander, Hiram, Barzillai, Lydia, and Philip William.

Margaret Mosher, of Barzillai, married Isaiah Miller, and had Barzillai, Mary Jane, and Amy Agnes.

Jehu Mosher, of Allen, he being of the Kempt family, married Esther Wilcox, Jr., and had the following children: — Jane, Byard, Adeline, Amelia Emma, Phoebe, Mary Matilda, and Amy.

Robert Mosher, of Allen, married Mercy Armstrong, and she died without issue. Robert's second wife was Lydia Francis, who had only one daughter named Mercy Ann.

Wilcox Mosher, of Allen, married Isabelle McDougall, and had the following children: — Allen, Robert, Mary, Margaret, Fanny, Jane, and Daniel.

Fanny Mosher, of Allen, married Caleb Lake, their children being, — Caleb, George, Sally, Fanny, Esther, and Benjamin, and several others.

Amy Mosher, of Allen, married William Henry, and had the following children: Elias, Allen, William, Charles, Esther, Phoebe, Loraine, Fanny, Temperance, and Mary.

Simon Mosher, of Allen, married Sarah Lyons, of Belfast, Maine. Had — Allen, Esther, Olive, Lydia Jane, and

Adeline Amelia. Simon and wife died of small-pox in Maine.

Benjamin Mosher, of Allen, married Isabel Lake, of Benjamin, and had the following children: — Allen, Benjamin, and William. Several died when young.

Allen Mosher, of Allen, married Eliza Jane Burgess, and had the following children: — George, Reuben, Louisa, Frederick, Augusta, Henry, Florence, and Thomas.

Polly Mosher, of Allen, married John McLellan, and had the following children: — John, Allen, Joseph, Lafayette, Robert, William, and Mrs. Hiltz. John McLellan, of Polly, was a sea-captain of note.

Rebecca Mosher, of Allen, married Stephen Lake, and had one girl, named Lydia. The mother died soon after this child was born.

Lydia Mosher, of Allen, married John Terhune, and had the following children: — Jehu, John, Allen, and Mary Matilda. Terhune died, and Lydia married - Marshall, and had two boys and one girl.

Rhoda Mosher, of Allen, married David Burgess, and had Ezekiel, Mary Jane, and Ruth. David died, and Rhoda married Arza Adus Wilcox, and had Lorenza, James, and Ira.

Jehu Mosher, of Nicholas and Polly, married Agnes Anthony, of Noah, and had Mary, Jacob, Agnes, and Archibald. They moved to Toronto in 1829. Later on Agnes (Jehu's wife) died, and Jehu married Delilah Smith, the second family consisting of John, Cyrus, Sarah, Harriet H., and Lydia. Jehu was a well-known and skilful mechanic.

He erected a number of saw and grist mills before leaving Nova Scotia, and followed the business in Ontario. Was also a wheelwright and general carpenter, and was called a very smart man. He died at a good old age at Mount Albert, Ontario, being over 87 years.

Rachel Mosher, of Nicholas and Polly, married Jacob Anthony, of Noah, and had Job, Levina, James William, Mary, Amy, Jane, Abigail, Noah, Jacob, and Nicholas. The latter was lost at sea.

Amy Mosher, of Nicholas and Polly, married Robert Ward, and had seven children, — Jehu, Mary, James, Nicholas, Simon, Abigail, and Elizabeth.

Mary Mosher, of Nicholas and Polly, married John Blois, and had Amy, Eliza, Abraham, Rachel, Polly, Lydia, and Jacob.

James Mosher, of Nicholas and Polly, married Martha Ward. Their children were, — Rhoda, Nicholas, John William, Mary Ann, Daniel, James, and George. In a few years Martha Ward died, and James married Catherine Ross, who had three children, — Jehu R., Martha, and Thomas.

Abigail Mosher, of Nicholas and Polly, married Increase Ward, and had Rachel, James, Thomas, Mary, Sarah Ann, Olive, Amy, and Martha.

Lydia Mosher, of Nicholas and Polly, married James Blois, and had Daniel, James, Nicholas, Cornelius Hiram, and Mary Maria.

Olive Mosher, of Nicholas and Polly, married Nathaniel O'Brien, and had Rebecca, Esther, Robert, Elizabeth, Catherine Ellis, Thomas Reid, William, and John Mosher.

Nicholas Mosher, of Nicholas and Polly, married Amy Harvie, and had Olive, Mary, Ann, Eleanor, and George Jehu.

George Mosher, of Nicholas and Polly, married Jane O'Brien, and had one daughter at the time they moved to Ontario, Canada, in 1829. In that province the following children were born to them: — Mary, Rebecca, Frances, Sarah Ann, and William. The latter died at the age of 19 years, at Rochester, N. Y. George also died there of consumption, brought on by exposure, about 1868. His wife, Jane, also died at Rochester in 1888. Rebecca, Frances, and Sarah Ann now live in the State of New York.

Tonge Mosher, of Nicholas and Polly, married Lucy Ward, and had Martha, James, Ward, Nicholas, Mary Ann, and John A. Some time after Lucy Ward died, and Tonge married Sophia Frizzle, who had one daughter, Rebecca.

Daniel Mosher, of Nicholas and Polly, married Elizabeth Mosher, of Nicholas, shipbuilder. Had no issue. She died of cancer.

John A. Mosher, of Nicholas and Polly, married Mary Ward, and had Minnie and Walter. The latter is a machinist, and is employed at the Woollen Mills, St. Croix, Hants Co. John A. is a millwright.

Elizabeth Mosher, of Nicholas and Polly, married Samuel Smith, a joiner by trade. They had four children — Mary Ann, Clarissa, Lydia, and Amy Eliza.

Sarah Mosher, of Nicholas and Polly, married David Smith, and had Eliza, Daniel W., Rachel, Mary Ann, Jane, and Catherine.

As will be observed, the above Nicholas and Polly had fifteen children. They all grew up and married, and Mrs. John Blois (Mary) died at the age of 44 years and 6 months. Mrs. Jacob Anthony (Rachel) died at the age of 59 years. Mrs. Samuel Smith (Elizabeth) died at the age of 62 years. The remainder that died lived from 65 to 87 years. Mrs. James Blois (Lydia) died June 22nd, 1886, aged 86 years. Daniel and John A. Mosher are living at this date, 1891; Daniel was 81 years in March, and John A. was 79 years last November.

James Mosher, of Joseph and Priscilla, married Rachel Lahey, and had Priscilla, James, Mary Ann, Barzillai, William, Joseph, John, Jehu, Charles, Harriet, and Rachel Catherine.

Barzillai Mosher, of Joseph, married Nancy Harvie, of Kennetcook, and had Catherine Ellis, Lydia Ann, Priscilia, Jennie, Jas. Barzillai, Alfred, William, and Adelaide. The above Barzillai was a ship-builder of note.

Daniel Mosher, of Joseph, married Jenny Ryan, and had Elizabeth, Priscilla, and James. Jennie died, Daniel taking for his second wife Margaret Ward, who had Daniel, Allen, Mary Ann, and Albert. Daniel lost his second wife, and married Jane McCoy, at Miramichi, N. B., and had Joseph, George, Robert, William, Hiram, Nathaniel, John, Rufus, Harriet Emma, and Margaret Ellen. Daniel was a very smart man, could do almost anything,— a good carpenter, blacksmith, quite a tailor, and a good shoemaker.

Elizabeth Mosher, of Joseph, married Reuben Mosher, of Jehu, and had Priscilla, Reuben, Joseph, Thomas, Daniel, James N., George, and Hannah.

Nicholas Mosher, of Joseph, married Fanny Young, and had Joseph, John, Priscilla, Sarah, Rachel, Harriet, William, David, George, James, Mark, Nicholas, and Ira. David went to sea. He sailed out of Walton, and as he was not heard of for many years, it is thought he was either lost at sea, or died in the West Indies. James died of fever in the West Indies.

Joseph Mosher, of Joseph, married Lydia Anthony, of Noah, and had William, Mahala, George, Noah, and Hiram. The above Joseph was a wheelwright and millwright, made all sorts of wheels, and was considered a superior workman.

Mary Mosher, of Joseph, married Captain George Card, and had Priscilla, Edward, Rachel Ann, Amy Elizabeth, George William, Margaret, James Hiram, Delina, and Fidelia. Edward was a sea-captain. He died in St. John, N. B., of ship fever. Priscilla married Capt. Rierson, of Eastport. Capt. Geo. Card was killed at Halifax by being caught between the mooring-post and a steamer, when raising the mooring-hawser over the post. He was a tide-waiter of the Customs.

William Mosher, of Joseph, never married, on account of ill-health. Died of kidney disease at Halifax, July, 1833, aged 30 years.

Amy Mosher, of Joseph, married Isaac Fish, a blacksmith at Scotch Village, Newport, and had Maria Ann,

Priscilla, James, Joseph, Elizabeth, William, Robert, Amy, Isaac, George, Emeline, and Harriet.

George Mosher, of Joseph, married Mary A. McNab, and had George William, Priscilla E., Ruth A., Joseph, Margaret A., Helen M., Frances A., and Ada.

As will be seen, Joseph and Priscilla had ten children, all of whom grew up and married, except William, as above stated. James died at Mosherville, aged 84 years. Barzillai died at Burlington, of consumption, aged 61 years. Daniel died at Gaspe, P. Q., of tumor in the stomach, aged 70 years. Elizabeth died at Newport, aged 89 years and 10 months. Nicholas died at Walton, Hants, aged 68 years. Joseph died at Mosherville, suddenly, aged 85 years and 4 months. Mary died at Eastport, Me., at her daughter's home, aged 83 years. George died at Presque Isle, Me. Just after retiring to bed, a blood-vessel broke, and the blood poured from his mouth, and he died in a few minutes. He was 64 years of age. Amy Fish still lives at Scotch Village, Newport, a fine looking old lady, in her 86th year.

William Mosher, of George and Margaret Thompson, married Eleanor Bennet, and had Leander, William, James, Nicholas, George, Ira, Pelina, Margaret, and Sophia.

Lydia Mosher, of George, married Richard Mounce, of England, and had William, Mary Ann, and George, who was a successful sea-captain, and now resides at Avondale, Hants Co. The above Richard Mounce was a miller by trade, and died at Annapolis.

Cyrus Mosher, of George, married Maria Fish, and had Isaac, Eliza, William, Margaret, and Maria Jane.

Eliza Mosher, of George, married Thomas Wallace, and had Eliza and Matilda, the mother dying soon after the birth of Matilda.

Darius Mosher, of Geo., married Susannah Burgess, and had James, Eliza, George, Mary, Selesta, Alfred, and Darius. Susannah died. Darius married Jane Hull Walker, for his second wife, and had William Tweedy, Margaret, and Maria.

Ira Mosher, of George, married Miss Teall, of St. John, N.B., and had Samuel T., Margaret, and William Henry. Mrs. Mosher died, and Ira married Catherine Chisholm, the second issue being, — Catherine, Hugh, and Sarah, all born in St. John. Ira and wife and the children of the second family moved to Avondale, Hants Co.

Nicholas Mosher, of Geo., married Jane Chambers, and had Arabella, Hugh, Albert, Louisa, Jane, and Roland M.

James Mosher, of George, also married, his children being, — James, Nicholas, Orris, Charlotte, and Catherine. Orris is a lawyer, located in Illinois.

Margaret Mosher, of George, married Elkanah Harvie, and had George Cyrus, Celesta, John Andrew, and Ira.

Nicholas Mosher, of George, was a ship-builder. He built many good vessels. The ship "Jenny Lind," the first full-rigged ship built and rigged out in Hants Co.; also the barque "Moro Castle," sailed for a time by Capt. James Mosher, ran as a packet carrying goods between London, G.B., and Halifax. Then sailed by Capt. Geo. Mounce for a time, who was very successful. The above Ira Mosher moved up from St. John to Avondale, to join his brother

Nicholas in ship-building. They launched the ship "Jenny Lind," and Ira went down in her to St. John, where she loaded. While there a ship came from Europe with many passengers, with ship fever on board. The vessel was quarantined. Many of the passengers died, and it is said that many were buried not a foot below the surface. When warm weather came, a friend of Ira's invited him to go out, and, as it was a short cut to cross this burial-ground, he went that way. He said the smell was dreadful while they crossed. He soon came home, took sick, and died in a few days. He and others believed the trip across the grounds caused his death. The above John Andrew, of Margaret, got the shipyard from his uncle Nicholas, and was a clever builder. He constructed many fine ships, and was always ready to adopt the latest improvements, and stood high as a citizen and ship-builder in the estimation of the public. He died of heart disease, aged 47 years. His brother-in-law was a partner with him. He (William H. Mosher) continued the business, and is noted for the building of fine vessels.

The above George Mosher had a farm within two miles of the place where his father landed, which was bounded on the north by the Kennetcook River. He had a large shop; was a wheelwright and general carpenter; kept several carpenters employed; ran a blacksmith shop to iron the work; had a number of apprentices; built the first waggon that was in the county, and his son Darius drove it, as he was a helper on the farm. It was rigged to be drawn by oxen or horses. Previous to this all used carts.

The said Darius lives on the farm now, is hale and hearty, and was 90 years old the 7th day of March, 1891. After a time George built small waggons to ride in to church. Also superintended the construction of King's College, Windsor.

The Eighth Generation

Alexander Mosher, of James, and grandson of Barzillai, married Hester Fish, and had James I., George, John, Olive, Loran, William, Margaret, Agnes, Charles, and Mary.

Barzillai Mosher, of James and Susannah, married Melina Miller (widow), and had Lewis, James A., and Levina.

Philip Mosher, of James and Susannah, married Eliza Brison (widow), and had Philip Earl, formerly engineer of the cotton mill, Windsor, but now in charge of the electric light station.

John Mosher, of James and Susannah, was a blacksmith, who died at the age of 33 years, and did not marry.

Sarah Mosher, of James and Susannah, married Sherbrooke Miller, and had Elias, Henry P., Barzillai, Heber, Annie, Mary, Charlotte, and Sophia.

Margaret, Mary Ann, and **Amy,** of James, did not marry.

Silas Mosher, of Jehu and Mary Burgess, married Martha Knowles, and had Sabra, Rebecca, William H., and Jehu.

Sarah Mosher, of Jehu and Mary, married John Armstrong, and had Silas, Mary Elizabeth, Frances Matilda, Thomas Henry, Melinda Ann, Elias Benjamin, Nicholas

James, John Murdock, William Summerville, Frank Roberts, Joseph Edwin, and Jehu Allen.

John Edward Mosher, of Jehu and Mary, married Rachel Sanford, and had Mary Matilda, Eunice, Sarah Jemima, and Hannah Priscilla.

Ann Mosher, of Jehu and Mary, married Campbell Church, and had George. He is a ship-carpenter, and lives in Newport.

Matilda Mosher, of Jehu and Mary, married Rev. Mr. Hennigar. No issue. She was his second wife.

Hannah Jane Mosher, of Jehu and Mary, married Frank Roberts. No issue.

Jehu Allen Mosher, of Jehu and Mary, married Tamer Constantine, and had James William and Alberta Mary. There were other children, who died young.

Ezekiel Mosher, of Jehu and Mary, married Olive Mosher, — of Nicholas (of Nicholas) and Amy Harvie, — and had Nettie and Mary, who are now with their mother in Newton, Mass. The above Nettie studied medicine, and got a diploma. Was also a writer of note. Resides in Massachusetts, U. S.

The above Ezekiel was a blacksmith, said to be a superior horseshoer and good general workman. He served his time with Elias Armstrong.

Hannah Mosher, of Daniel and Lavinia Black, married Girden Macumber, and had George, John, Daniel, and Nicholas. Girden died, and Hannah married Joseph Longstaff, and had by Longstaff the following: — Lavina, Eliza, and Margaret.

Jehu Mosher, of Daniel and Lavinia, married Sarah Wilson, and had Sarah J., Mary M., Elizabeth E., Satira M., Agnes E., Lavinia L., and Joseph William.

Eliza Mosher, of Daniel and Lavinia, married Reid Monroe, and had William, James, Daniel, Edwin, Samuel, Annie, Mary, EUie, and Ida.

Matilda Mosher, of Daniel and Lavinia, married Abraham Wilson, and died without issue.

Reuben Mosher, of Daniel and Lavinia, is a bachelor.

Daniel Archibald Mosher, of Daniel and Lavinia, married Esther Meharg, their issue being, — Geo. Brown, Jehu Edward, Archibald Grant, Florence, Lilly, and Maud.

John Barzillai Mosher, of Daniel and Lavinia, married Isabella Thompson, their children being, — William, Reuben, Senaca, David, Clara Alberta, Edith Agerta, and Estella Satira.

Sarah Mosher, of Daniel and Lavinia, married Samuel Carson, and had Daniel A., Robert J., Mary J., and Sarah A.

William Mosher, of Daniel and Lavinia, died under age.

The above family live in Brockway Centre, St. Clair County, Michigan.

Lemina Mosher, of James and Mary Smith, married John Marsters, and had James, Leonard, Abraham, Samuel, Edward, Adeline, Julia, and Mary.

Matilda Mosher, of Jas. and Mary, married Edward McDonald, and had James, Frank, Loran, Mary, Julia, Hannah, and Caroline.

Daniel Mosher, of James and Mary, married Mary Alice Fox, and had John E. F., James Harding, Howard Hooper, Annabelle, Essie, Frederick Otto, Alice, and. Francis.

Thomas Harding Mosher, of James and Mary, married Julia Walker, of Chester. The family is in Boston, Mass. Thomas died there.

Lydia Ann Mosher, of James, did not marry; lives in Boston.

James Allen Mosher, of James, married Julia E. Murphy, in Boston. James died at Boston, leaving a family. He was a blacksmith.

Calvin Smith Mosher, of James and Mary, married Augusta L.A. Wild, of Baltimore, Md., and had Minnie, Adam and Hugh.

Several children of Calvin are highly educated, and Calvin is Secretary of the Prohibition Party of Maryland, auxiliary to the National Prohibition Party.

James Mosher, of Nicholas and Nancy Malcom, married Hannah Sell Fish, and had Joan, Henry, Frederick, and Hannah Sell. Hannah (James' wife) died, and he married Maria Woolaver, and had Thomas A., Annie Maria, and Arthur. The latter died in his 27th year, at Avondale.

Melinda Mosher, of Nicholas and Nancy, married Capt. Thomas H. Armstrong, and had Ann and Olivia. Capt. Armstrong died at sea, and Olivia died at Avondale, soon after arriving at womanhood.

Sarah Jane Mosher, of Nicholas and Nancy, married Capt. Frederick Curry, a very successful ship-master. They had Mary, Nicholas, Frederick, and Rufus.

The above Nicholas was a sea-captain, and sailed some of his father's ships.

Nicholas Mosher, of Nicholas and Nancy, married Ann Davis, and had Thomas Davis, Walter Palmer, Rupert James, Gibson Clark, and Howard Allen.

The above Nicholas was a ship-builder, and built several ships for Capt. F. Curry. He died of heart disease, suddenly.

Elizabeth Mosher, of Nicholas and Nancy, married Daniel Mosher, of Nicholas and Polly. Had no issue. Elizabeth died of cancer.

Margaret M. Mosher, of Nicholas and Nancy, married J. W. Allison, a merchant and postmaster of Newport Landing. Margaret died without issue in 1882, aged 56 years.

Hannah Mosher, of Nicholas and Nancy, married Rev. John A. Mosher (of Allen), and had Annie Draper and Fred. Thornton.

Matilda Mosher, of Nicholas and Nancy, did not marry. She lived in part of her father's house at Avondale.

Daniel Mosher, of Nicholas and Nancy, married Merinda Martin, their issue being, — Nicholas, Frederick, William, Daniel Alston, Annie Rachel, Newton Etter, and Malcolm. Daniel is a farmer, and lives on part of the old homestead of his grandfather, Jehu Mosher, near where his great-grandfather landed.

James Taylor Mosher, of Allen and Jennie Proctor, married Fannie Card. They had one son, Israel, who fell from a stage in Bennett Smith's shipyard, and was killed, at the age of 21 years.

William Mosher, of Allen and Jennie, married Catherine Smith, and had Whidden, Morris, Lorette, Allen, Wesley, and Hattie.

John A. Mosher, of Allen and Jennie, married Hannah Mosher (of Nicholas and Nancy), their issue being Annie Draper and Fred. Thornton.

Olive Mosher, of Allen and Jennie, married William Forrest, and had two children, both of whom died young. William was a ship-carpenter.

Melinda Jane Mosher, of Allen and Jennie, married Job Harvie. They have one daughter, Jane Harvie, who is in her teens.

Priscilla Mosher, of Reuben and Elizabeth Mosher, married Ramsey Hunter, and had James, Reuben, Thomas and Walter.

Reuben Mosher, of Reuben and Elizabeth, married Ann Crossley, and had I. Ulus Crossley, Mary Elizabeth, Priscilla Ann, James Aeneas, Ramsey Hunter, Thomas Allen, George William, Edwin Card and Edgar Delancey. The last two are twins.

Joseph Mosher, of Reuben and Elizabeth, married Melinda Greeno (widow), and had Major Mosher, who was a successful ship-master. He died at Avondale, 1890, leaving no issue, aged 42 years.

Daniel Mosher, of Reuben and Elizabeth, married Martha Constantine. They had Johnston arid Newton. Martha died, and Daniel married Mary Ann Crowell, a widow. No issue.

James N. Mosher, of Reuben and Elizabeth, married Anna Greeno, and had Bessie Albina, Major G., Henrietta Morton, Judson Fox, and Egbert Haldane.

George Mosher, of Reuben and Elizabeth, married Martha Cox. No issue. George afterwards married Caroline McDonald, who had Charles and Percy. The latter was adopted by Capt. Major Mosher.

Hannah Mosher, of Reuben and Elizabeth, married Robert O'Brien, and had Bessie, Joseph and Eliza. Robert died, and in a few years Hannah died also. The son Joseph died under age.

Rachel Salome Mosher, of Noah and Eliza Stilman, married a Mr. Dutcher, of New York, and had Angeline. They live in New York.

Omen Edward Mosher, of Noah and Eliza, married, and has a family in Bridgeport, Connecticut.

Damarius Mosher, of Noah and Eliza, married a Mr. Fisher, and had Leander and Augusta.

Leander Mosher, of Noah and Eliza, married, and had a family in New York. Leander died some years ago.

Noah Mosher, of Noah and Eliza, married, and has a family in New York.

Clementina Mosher, of Noah and Eliza, married a Mr. Briggs, and has a family in New York.

The above family moved from Avondale to Bridgeport, and Noah died suddenly a few years ago, in his chair, of heart trouble.

Annet Mosher, of Captain Nelson and Margaret Murphy, did not marry, and is now living in Boston.

Ellen Mosher, of Nelson and Margaret, married Richard Eagles. They have five children, and are living in Boston.

Margaret Mosher, of Nelson and Margaret, married Frederick Coon. They have two children, now living with their parents in Boston.

Narraway Mosher, of Nelson and Margaret, married in Quebec, and had three children. He (Narraway) was a sea-captain. While on a voyage from England to the United States, his wife and two children being in the ship with him, his vessel was lost with all on board. One daughter was left in Quebec with her grandparents.

Lilly Vivian Mosher, of Nelson and his second wife Catharine, married Alpheus Harvie, of Ira, their children being Nelson and Ira Wilbert.

Almona Mosher, of Nelson and Catherine, married Annie Anderson, of Cape Breton. Their children were Harry McKewen and Luby, who are now living in Boston.

Nelson Mosher, of William and Mary Bell, married Maria Mosher, of Darius. Their only child was Charles Mosher. After Maria's death, which occurred when this child was about a year old. Nelson married Florence Chambers, and has a family in California.

Ovilla Mosher, of George Hiram and Mary Warnock, married a soldier at Halifax and went away.

Orilla Mosher, of George H. and Mary, married James Embree and had five children — Nelson, Ethel, Orman, Elmer, and Lestra.

Major Mosher, of George H. and Mary, married Lilla Desby, and had three children, Pansie P., and Mary, now living in Boston.

Georgia Mosher, of George H. and Mary, married Darius Mosher, their children being Maria Josephine, Maggie Malcom, Clarence E., Loran Chambers, Persie A. and Ethel Mary.

Clementine Mosher, of George H. and Mary, married E. C. Embree, at Port Hawksbury, Nov. 19th, 1890.

Eighth Generation— Continued.

Kempt Family

Byard Mosher, of Jehu and Esther Wilcox, Jr., married Sarah Jane Galbraith, and had ten children — Seward, Martha Jane, John Fulton, Esther, Eliza, Mary Matilda, Thomas Byard, Jehu Andrew, George William and James Robert.

Allen Mosher, of Wilcox and Isabel McD., married Elizabeth McDougall, and had William Allen, Ancey, and Sarah Elizabeth.

Allen B. Mosher, of Benjamin and Isabel Lake, married Frances Lake. Their children were — William Darius, Rachel Ann, Sarah Jestina, Terrence, and Sarah Alice.

William Mosher, of Benjamin and Isabel, married Mary Dearman, and has no issue.

Mercy Ann Mosher, of Robert and Lydia Francis, married H. A. Brown, and had George Arnold, Emma Marion and Amy Helen McLean.

George Mosher, of Allen and Eliza J. Burgess, married Abigail Macomber, by whom he had Bessie, Annie, and Walter. On the death of his wife, Abigail, George married Matilda Macumber, at Newport, and she died without issue. George then married Amelia McCallum, whose children were Matilda and Gertrude.

Frederick Mosher, of Allen and Eliza, married Annie Scott, and had seven children, — Conman, Frank, Hollis, Eugenia, Edith, Ethel, and Elizabeth.

Henry Mosher, of Allen and Eliza, named Rose Bradshaw, and had Winnie, Rose, Gladys and Dora.

Thomas Mosher, of Allen and Eliza, married Alena Sanford. Their children are Leila, Laura, and a baby girl.

Reuben Mosher, of Allen and Eliza, married Ann Gray, and had Ida, Edward, and William.

Flora Mosher, of Allen and Eliza, married William Wood, and has no issue.

Augusta Mosher, of Allen and Eliza, married Wm. Sanford. After the birth of a son, William, the family moved to Boston.

Louisa Mosher, of Allen and Eliza, married James Tracy. They are living in Windsor.

Abigail Mosher, of Allen and Eliza, married George Scott. Their children are — Walter, Eva, and Alice. Mr. Scott is now dead.

Jane Mosher, of Jehu and Esther Wilcox, Jr., married

Capt. John McLellan. Their children are — Jehu, Emma, Eleanor, George, Jane Fulton, Annie, and John.

Adeline Mosher, of Jehu and Esther, married Capt. Daniel McKenzie, and had two daughters, who grew to womanhood and died. The mother, Adeline, died at Summerville, Hants, of heart disease, in 1890.

Amelia Emma Mosher, of Jehu and Esther, married Capt. Elisha Francis, and had one son, Kelsie Francis. Her husband, Elisha, was lost at sea, all hands perishing with him.

Amy Mosher, of Jehu and Esther, married Capt. H. H. Greeno, a very successful ship-master, at Cheverie, Hants.

Martha Mosher, of Wilcox and Isabella McD., married Allen Lake, and had Martha and Allen. After Allen's death, Martha married Stephen Brown, their children being — Frederick, Jane, Emma, Annie, Isaac, Lolo,. John Albert, Isabella, and Ezariah.

Mary Mosher, of Wilcox and Isabella, married Allen McLellan, and has no issue.

Jane Mosher, of Wilcox, married G. Fisher, and has no issue.

Margaret Mosher, of Wilcox and Isabella, married George Winters, and had Elizabeth, Eleanor, and Jane.

Fanny Mosher, of Wilcox, married Henry Lake. They had two daughters, Eleanor and Jane.

Priscilla Mosher, of James and Rachel, married Columbus Wier, and had the following children: — James, Daniel, Nelson, Rachel, Joseph, Hiram, John, Margaret, Mary, Lucinda, and Annie. One of the above, James Wier, recently deceased, was a successful doctor, practising at the head of Kennetcook. Another son, Nelson Wier, is a J. P., Clerk of Municipal Council, and keeps a grocery and general store at the head of Kennetcook, Hants.

James Mosher, of James and Rachel, married Mary Clark, by whom he had the following children: — Rufus C, Pauline, James D., Ira M., and Matilda. The second son, James D. Mosher, is an M. D., and is practising medicine at Rawdon, Hants Co. Ira M. Mosher is a sea-captain, now commanding the ship "Sultan." The father, James, was a sea-captain, and was one of our first deep-water captains. He commanded the ship "Moro Castle," which ran for a time between London and Halifax, and was built by Nicholas Mosher (of George) at Avondale, Hants Co.

Mary Ann Mosher, of James and Rachel, married Joseph Carter, of Rawdon, and had the following children: — Charles, Hannah, and William. The latter died young.

Barzillai Mosher, of James and Rachel, was one of the crew of the brig "Leone." The ship and all hands were lost, April, 1845.

William Mosher, of James and Rachel, married Lucinda Burgess, William was lost in the brig "Geo. M. Sole," Capt. Harvie, in 1846, leaving no issue. The brig was never heard of after leaving Liverpool, G. B.

Joseph Mosher, of James and Rachel, married Asenath Anthony. He died of tumor in the stomach, leaving no issue.

John Mosher, of James and Rachel, died at home, unmarried, at the age of 23 years.

Jehu Mosher, of James and Rachel, married Jane Anthony (of Jacob), and had no issue. He died of dropsy in 1887.

Charles Mosher, of James and Rachel, married Jane Hall, at Canso, N.S., and had the following children: — Alfred Stevens, Clarissa, Edgar, Eugenia, and Rachel Harriet. Charles lives in King's County, N.S.

Harriet Mosher, of James and Rachel, married William Mosher (of Joseph), and had one son, Austin, who was married June 3rd, 1890, to the widow Harvie, daughter of William Murphy, Esq., of Newport. The above Austin is Montreal correspondent to the Toronto *Empire,* the Government paper of the day. He has a thorough knowledge of the French language, as well as his own tongue, and as he resides in the French district of Montreal, he is enabled to send news from this part of the city, written in English, for the benefit of the readers of the "Empire."

Rachel C. Mosher, of James and Rachel, was never married, and died at home of brain fever, aged 25 years.

Catherine Ellis Mosher, of Barzillai and Nancy, married Capt. John Mann, and had but one son, James, who was a successful sea-captain, and died in Liverpool, England, of enlargement of the heart, in 1879. He was master of the barque "Anglesea," built by John A. Harvie, at Avondale, Hants County. Capt. James left a young widow, one daughter and two sons, now living at Burlington, Hants Co., N. S.

Lydia Ann Mosher, of Barzillai and Nancy, married Capt. John Liswell, and had the following children: —

James William, Emma Malissa, and Ellen, who died young. James W. Liswell is a sea-captain, and is now master of ship "Mark Curry," launched at Avondale, Nov. 26th, 1890. Her husband, Capt. John Liswell, was master of the brig "Leone," lost on the passage from Windsor to New York, with all hands, eight in number, including Capt. Liswell. The ship was last seen beating out the South Channel, April, 1845.

Priscilla Mosher, of Barzillai and Nancy, married Capt. Joshua Francis, and had one son, Lewis, who died at Havana, West Indies, of yellow fever. He was mate with his father. Priscilla died in Philadelphia of diarrhoea. Her husband was with her at the time of her death.

Jenny Mosher, of Barzillai and Nancy, married John G. Kirkpatrick, and died within a year, leaving an infant.

James Barzillai Mosher, of Barzillai and Nancy, was lost with Capt. Liswell in the brig "Leone." He was a young man not quite of age.

William Mosher, of Barzillai and Nancy, married Rosalina Hatch, daughter of Capt. Hatch, of Portland, Me. They had one son, the mother dying when the boy was quite young. The child went to live with his grandfather. His father was a sea-captain, sailing out of Portland, which is all that the writer knew of him.

Adelaide Mosher, of Barzillai and Nancy, married Ezekiel Lake. Her children were — Barzillai, Alalia, Manning and Charles.

Mrs. Mann, Mrs. Liswell and Mrs. Lake reside in Burlington, Hants County, within a mile of where they were born.

Elizabeth Mosher, of Daniel and Jenny, married Capt. Vance, of Eastport, Me., and had two children. They both died young. Capt. Vance was drowned, and his widow, Elizabeth, married a man by the name of Baris, by whom she had one daughter, and after a few years she died at Calais, Me.

Priscilla Mosher, of Daniel and Jenny, married Capt. Flood, who was afterwards drowned. They had one daughter, Louisa, who grew up and married in Calais, Me.

James Mosher, of Daniel and Jenny, never married, and died of consumption at Gaspe, in the Province of Quebec, where he was living with his half-sister. He was a very intelligent man, and an excellent carpenter.

Daniel Mosher, of Daniel and Margaret, married in Calais, had a family, and died some years ago. He had a brother, Allen, who died unmarried. Also a brother Albert, who died in Calais, aged about 21.

Mary Ann Mosher, of Daniel and Margaret, went to Gaspe with her father, and married Capt. John Ascah at Gaspé. She had no issue, and still lives in Gaspé.

Joseph Mosher, of Daniel and Jane McCoy, his last wife, sailed out of Quebec a few years, but left there some ten years ago. His friends have not heard of him since.

George Mosher, of Daniel and Jane, married Ellen Cunning, by whom he had the following: Joseph, Robert,

George, Harvie, Miles, Henry, and Jesse. George and his wife are both dead, the former dying in Toronto in 1890.

William Mosher, of Daniel and Jane McCoy, married Ann Emery (widow), whose maiden name was Davis, their children being — Sarah, Priscilla, Carrie, Harriet Emma, Annie, Ellen, and Janet.

Hiram Mosher, of Daniel and Jane, married Eliza Emery, and had Mary Ann, Allen, James Harriet, Arthur, William, Austin, and Roy Emery.

John Mosher, of Daniel and Jane, married an American woman — a widow — and has no issue.

Robert Mosher, of Daniel and Jane, is sailing a steamboat at Port Francis, and has a family there.

Nathaniel Mosher, of Daniel, is with Robert, and also has a family.

Rufus Mosher, of Daniel and Jane, is not married. He was in Minnesota lumber woods in 1888.

Harriet Emma Mosher, of Daniel and Jane, married George Miller, at Gaspé and had one son, Wilbert Austin. His mother died when he was three weeks old. He (W. Austin) is in Gaspé, and is a young man about twenty years of age.

Margaret Ellen Mosher, of Daniel and Jane, married David Rabey. Their children are — Ida Jane, Eliza Ann, Ellen Jemima, Harriet Emma, and David Daniel.

Joseph Mosher, of Nicholas and Fanny Walker, married Lucy Clark, of Walton, N.S., and had Levina, Harriet, Lucy, and George. He died at Truro, of consumption. On the death of Lucy, Joseph's wife, he married Rebecca

Carmichael, by whom he had Herbert Silas, Joseph Stanley, and Minnie Laura. Joseph now lives in East Saginaw, Michigan, U.S.

John Mosher, of Nicholas and Fanny, married Sarah Greeno, and had Emma, Sylvias, Prescott, Matilda, Ada, Harry Herminius, Mary, Trask, and Jeremiah.

Priscilla Mosher, of Nicholas and Fanny, married Samuel Davis. Their children are — Joseph, David, James, Sarah, Nicholas, Sabra, and Clara.

Sarah Mosher, of Nicholas and Fanny, married James Jacobs, of Portland, Me., and had four children, — James, Mary, Perry, and David.

Rachel Mosher, of Nicholas and Fanny, married John Clifford, and has no issue. They live in Maine, U. S.

Harriet Mosher, of Nicholas and Fanny, married Robert McLellan, and had Sarah Hannah, George Wm., John Timothy, Susan Frances, Clara H., Nicholas M., Robert G., James Whidden, and Andrew A. Robert and Harriet are now living in Brooklyn, Hants.

Nicholas Mosher, of Nicholas and Fanny, married Eliza Smith, their children being: Wesley, George, Francis, Trask, Edward, Albert, Annie, and Minnie. Some years ago Nicholas went, to California, in search of employment, intending to send for his family after he was settled. While there, he died under very sad circumstances. While crossing a bay with a ship deeply laden, it filled with water and sank. He swam ashore, but was so chilled and exhausted that he died before he could reach a house only a quarter of a mile a day.

Mark Mosher, of Nicholas and Fanny, married Lucy Ettinger, by whom he had Carrie and two other children. They are now living in Portland, Me.

Margaret Mosher, of Nicholas and Fanny, married Alexander Tobin, a sea-captain, and had Fanny, Edward, and William. Tobin was lost in the brig "Ada," and all hands with him. After his death, Margaret married John Campbell, their children being, — George, John, Rachel, Durney, and two girls.

Ira Mosher, of Nicholas and Fanny, married Matilda Scott, and had William, Laura, John, Fred, James, Alberta, and Carrie.

William Mosher, of Nicholas and Fanny, married Rachel Miller, and left no issue. He died in Portland, several years ago.

David Mosher, of Nicholas and Fanny, died of fever at sea. James and George went to sea. We have no account of what happened to them. Nicholas, father of the above, was a carpenter. He died in Walton, Hants County.

William Mosher, of Joseph and Lydia, married Harriet Mosher, and had one son, Austin, who lives in Montreal, and is a great politician. The above William Mosher was a shipbuilder and draughtsman. He draughted the barque "Boaz," (round stern), which was among the first round stern vessels built in Avondale. He draughted the ship in full, giving the bevels of every timber for the first time in Hants County. In building round sterns before, it was customary to make a skeleton of the stern trimmed to get the bevels by a bevel. This was about 1864. Shipbuilding in Hants has taken great strides since that date.

Mahala Mosher, of Joseph and Lydia, married Andrew Anthony, and had three children: — Cinderella E., Benjamin, and Delina M.

George Mosher, of Joseph and Lydia, married Mary O. Smith, by whom he had Emeline, Otis B., Lydia Elvira, Whidden, and Blanche. Above George is a carpenter and spar-maker.

Noah Mosher, of Joseph and Lydia, married Annie R. Clark, and had Linden, Brenton, Valentine, Lydia, Emily, and Everett. He is a first-class ship-carpenter.

Hiram Mosher, of Joseph and Lydia, married Mary Ann Smith, and had Bertha, Ella, and Phebe. He is a carpenter.

Agnes Mosher, of Jehu and Agnes Anthony, married Benj. Burns. Their children are — George W., Matilda Ann, Sarah E., Hannah H., Zilpha E., William M., Clark, Howard, and Clara Bell Burns.

Archibald Mosher, of Jehu and Agnes, married Annie Marshall, and had Agnes Ann, Mary Jane, Bertha Gertrude, and Elizabeth. Archibald died in Toronto in 1888.

Jacob Mosher, of Jehu and Agnes, removed many years ago to Minnesota, where he married a widow, name unknown. They had three children. He sold his farm in Minnesota and moved away, and has not been heard of for many years.

Nicholas Mosher, of James and Martha Ward, married Catherine Frizzle, and had two daughters — Fannie and Georgia.

Mary Ann Mosher, of James and Martha, married Henry Ross, and had four children: — Frederick Mosher, James Ramsey, Josephine Martha, and Annie Bancroft.

Daniel Mosher, of James and Martha, married Ann Spence, and had two sons — Andrew James and Marshall. The youngest, Marshall, studied medicine. He obtained a diploma, and is now practising in Boston. After Ann's death, Daniel married Eliza Payzantson, and moved to Boston, where he died in 1887, leaving no issue by Eliza. She and Andrew James are now residing in Boston.

Jehu Ross Mosher, of James and Catherine Ross, married Cassandra Shaffelburg. Their children are — Florence, Frederick, and Cassandra. His wife (Cassandra) dying, Jehu married the widow Mosher, daughter of Lockhart Fox, by whom he had no issue. Jehu was a carpenter and a machinist, and was employed by Moir, the baker, in his mill at the head of Bedford Basin.

Martha Mother, of James and Catherine, married John Spruce, at Halifax Railway Depot, their children being Thomas, Nettie and John.

Thomas Mosher, of James and Catherine, married and lives in Lowell, Mass., where they have a family.

Olive Mosher, of Nicholas and Amy Harvie, married Ezekiel Mosher, of Jehu and Mary. They have two daughters, Nettie and Mary.

Mary Mosher, of Nicholas and Amy, never married, and is now living at Newton, Mass.

Ann Mosher, of Nicholas and Amy, married Jacob Millen and had nine children, — Laura B., Amy A., George M.,

Mattie E., Mary L., Ernest F., Olivia H., Nicholas S. and Rufus H.

Eleanor Mosher, of Nicholas and Amy, married Abraham Marsters. Their children are, — Kenneth N., Daniel M. and Lemina A.

George J. Mosher, of Nicholas and Amy, married Matilda Clark, by whom he had Joseph F., Horace G., Rebecca, Nicholas, John and Ira. On the death of his wife, Matilda, George J. married Lucinda Wier, and had two children, — Eugene and Amy.

James Mosher, of Tonge and Lucy, married Margaret Stone, their children being Frank and Lucy. The family now live in California.

Nicholas T. Mosher, of Tonge and Lucy, married Belinda Crossley, and had four children, — Ferdinand, Mary, Ward and Alice.

Martha Mosher, of Tonge and Lucy, married Edward McDonald. Her children are Tonge Mosher and Thomas.

Mary Ann Mosher, of Tonge and Lucy, married Thomas Warr, and had six children: — Francis, William, Maud, Thomas, Mary and Rose.

John A. Mosher, of Tonge and Lucy, married Sarah Pemberton, by whom he had Rachel, Lucy, Minnie, and Maud. John Mosher is a Justice of the Peace and a Councillor of Windsor, Hants County.

Walter Mosher, of John and Mary Ward, married Emma Sweet, and had two children — Robert and Lora. He is a machinist, employed in the St. Croix Woollen Mills.

Leander Mosher, of William and Eleanor Bennet, married Miss Long. He had nine children, five girls and four boys.

James Mosher, of William and Eleanor, is now living in Woburn, Mass. He has one son and one daughter.

William Mosher, of William and Eleanor, is married and in the whaling business. He has not been in Nova Scotia for over twenty years, and was last heard from in 1888.

Nicholas Mosher, of William and Eleanor, married Miss Patterson. He is now living in New Hampshire, and has a family there.

George Mosher, of William and Eleanor, married Miss Neville. They have one daughter, Dora, who is married. They live at Beech Hill, near Kentville, King's County, N.S. George's father died near there. He was a' wheelwright, and a superior turner of wood and iron.

Ira Mosher, of William and Eleanor, married the widow Mosher, of Newport, and had no issue. They moved to Bath, Me., where she died of measles soon after their arrival. Ira afterwards married Miss Forrest, by whom he had one son, Cyrus, now living in Boddingham. Me. Ira was a first-class mechanic, and a carpenter of note.

Pelina Mosher, of William and Eleanor, married Abner Schofield, and had a large family.

Margaret Mosher, of William and Eleanor, married Charles Jones, and had a large family.

Sophia Mosher, of William and Eleanor, married Charles Walton, and had no issue.

Isaac Mosher, of Cyrus and Maria Fish, never married. He followed the sea for many years, and died of small-pox in Philadelphia.

William Mosher, of Cyrus and Maria, was a blacksmith by trade. He married Margaret Malita Miller, and had one son. Miller Mosher. William died young.

Eliza Mosher, of Cyrus and Maria, married Thomas Miller, and had one son, John Levi, who was elected Councillor for West Hants in 1890.

Margaret Mosher, of Cyrus and Maria, married James Scott, and had two sons — Cyrus and Cameron.

Maria Jane Mosher, of Cyrus and Maria, married Capt. Eleazer Lockhart, of Avondale, Hants County, and has no issue.

James Mosher, of Darius and Susannah Burgess, married Hannah Jane Burgess, and had four children: — Edward, Ellmore, Georgia, and Margaret Ann.

George Mosher, of Darius and Susannah, married Ruby Ann Burgess, by whom he had Richard, Annie E., Emma M., Pauline, Sarah A., Cyrus G., Martin, and Watson.

Mary E. Mosher, of Darius and Susannah, married William Brison. Their children were: — Phebe B., James M., Bessie M., Murdock L., Darius M., and Henry W.

Alfred Mosher, of Darius and Susannah, married Margaret Dodge, and had one son, Laurie Alfred.

Selesta Mosher, of Darius and Susannah, married John Walker, and had John, Henry, Darius, William, Beatrice, and Maria.

Darius Mosher, of Darius and Susannah, married Georgia Mosher. Their children are, — Persie, Maria, Maggie, Clarence, Loran, and a baby girl.

William Tweedy Mosher, of Darius and Jane Hull, is unmarried.

Margaret Mosher, of Darius and Jane, married Richard Brison, and had two daughters. She died of consumption.

Maria Mosher, of Darius and Jane, married Nelson Mosher, (of William and Mary Bell), and had one son, Charles. She, too, died of consumption. Nelson afterwards married Florence Chambers, and moved to California.

Samuel Theall Mosher, of Ira and Miss Theall, married Rachel Ponsford Dunham, of St. John, N. B., and had Emma, who died in her teens, Sarah Theall, John Henry, George William, Gertrude Elizabeth, Mary Ethel, Ira, Abbie Corum, Amelia Dunham, and Annie Louisa.

Margaret Ann Mosher, of Ira and Miss Theall, married Thomas Alexander McMackin, of St. John, N.B. Their children are, — Frederick, Ernest, Jennie, Thomas Ira, J. Arthur, Emma Mosher, Fannie, Walter and Rubina Chisholm.

William Henry Mosher, of Ira and Miss Theall, married Annie Morrison, and had three children: William, Ira, and Margaret.

Hugh Mosher, of Ira and Catherine Chisholm, marricvA ,arah Jane Warnick, by whom he had Sarah Louisa, Harry Albert, and Maud Edna. Hugh lives in California, where he deals in fruit, has a fine fruit garden, and is doing a large business. His two sisters died of consumption.

Arabella Mosher, of Nicholas and Jane Chambers, married George N. Knowles. Their children are: Louisa Adele, Maud Arabella, Emma Tupper, and Alice Jane.

Hugh Mosher, of Nicholas and Jane, died of consumption on board brig "Relief." His death took place in Havanna, where he had gone hoping it would be a benefit to his health. ,

Albert Mosher, of Nicholas and Jane, married Jane Smith, and had Hubert G., and Eva and Eda (twins). After Jane died, Albert married Cinnie Bishop in Texas. Alberta is their only child. They now live in California.

Jane Mosher, of Nicholas and Jane, married John Kennedy. Their five children are: Sylvia Snow, Florence Alcott, Ethel, Globe Pierce, and Rocky Mountains.

Roland Morton Mosher, of Nicholas and Jane, married a widow with one daughter. Roland now lives in Prescott, the capital of Arizona, with his wife, step-daughter and his own two daughters.

The family of James Mosher, the brother of Nicholas, live in Kansas, whence they moved from Ontario, Canada,, some years ago.

James I. Mosher, of Alexander and Hester Fish, mavried Sophia Miller and had one daughter, Lavinia. After Sophia's death James married Clara Wier, who had no issue.

George Mosher, of Alexander and Hester, married Charlotte Fox and had two children, Bessie and Edward. George died some years after. None of his children are now living.

John Mosher, of Alexander and Hester, married Mary Vaughan, and had George, Emma, Annie, and a baby boy.

Loran Mosher, of Alexander and Hester, married Amelia Knowles, their children being William, Roy, and Grace.

Olive Mosher, of Alexander and Hester, married John Harvie, blacksmith. Her children are George, Etta, Norman, and Lewis.

Margaret Mosher, of Alexander and Hester, married James Pemberton, and had two sons, — Charles and Arthur.

Agnes Mosher, of Alexander and Hester, married Mr. Long, and had one son, Arthur. Being left a widow, she afterwards married Samuel Foss. No children have been born of the second marriage.

Mary Mosher, of Alexander and Hester, married Edward Worcester, and has no issue.

Philip Earl Mosher, of Philip and Eliza Brison, married Ella McDonald, who had one daughter, Gertrude. After Ella's death, Philip married Dora Davis, by whom he had Carl Grey and Philip Earl.

James A. Mosher, of Barzillai and Melina Miller, married Regina Marsters, and had two children, Nettie May and Wilfred Laurence.

Lewis Mosher, of Barzillai and Melina, married Annie Johnston in 1890. They have no children.

Lavina Mosher, of Barzillai and Melina, married William Carter, a blacksmith. They live in Brooklyn, Hants County, and have no issue.

Mary Mosher, of Nicholas and Belinda, married Edward Banks. Their children are: — Georgia, Edwin, and Cora.

Alice Mosher, of Nicholas and Belinda, married Gilbert Travis, and have two sons, Bertram and Edwin.

Ferdinand Mosher, of Nicholas and Belinda, married Christina Craig, of Belgium, G.B., and has no issue. Ferdinand is a sea-captain of note.

Ward Mosher, of Nicholas and Belinda, married Emma Grace Harvie, and has no issue. He is a cabinetmaker, and works in Windsor Furniture Factory.

Rachel Mosher, of John A. Mosher and Sarah Pemberton, married Ernest Marshall Bancroft. They have one son. Clarence Mosher.

Hannah Priscilla Mosher, of John Edward and Rachel Sanford, married George McNutt. Their children are: — Edward Emmerson, Charles Morton, Fulton Dexter, Rachel Elena, Frederick Sterns, Walter G., Harry M., Maud A., and Mabel Rose.

Sarah Jemima Mosher, of John E, and Rachel, married Capt. Daniel Dexter, of barque "Emma Payzant." Their children are: — Rachel Paul, ne and Mabel Rose.

Mary Matilda Mosher, of John E. and RacheJ, married D. C. Morgan, and has no issue.

Eunice Mosher, of John E. and Rachel, is living in Massachusetts, unmarried.

David B. Mosher, married Lydia Campbell, and had Orilla, Louisa, Nathaniel J., and Morris.

William H. Mosher, of Silas and Martha Knowles, married Isabella Briden, of St. John, N. B. They have five children: — John Andrew, Jessie, Francis William, Hugh Edward, and Waldo Elliott.

Sabra Mosher, of Silas and Martha, married John A. Harvie, ship-builder, their children being: — Silas Trask, Stafford Knowles, and Strothard Stanley.

Rebecca Mosher, of Silas and Martha, married Capt. George Mounce, and had Georgia and William. Rebecca died, and George Mounce married Annie Armstrong, and had two sons, Thomas Henry and Ralph.

Jehu Mosher, of Silas and Martha, married Eva Chambers. Their children are: — Frederick and Minnie Rebecca.

James William Mosher, of Jehu A. and Tamer Constantine, married Mary Morris. Their children are: Albert Cecil, Ralph Gordon, and Wiley Earl.

Alberta Mosher, of Jehu A. and Tamer, married William Brown, and has one son, Frederick.

Miller Mosher, of William and Margaret M. Miller, married Elizabeth Hunter, (one of the triplets of Guy), and had one son, Charles Mosher, who resides at St. Croix, Hants.

John E. F. Mosher, of Daniel and Mary Alice Fox, married Rebecca Murphy, (of Capt. Thomas), and had six sons: — James Lemont, Thos. Nelson, Daniel Gilbert, Charles Roland, John Clifford, and Harry Farnsworth.

James Harding Mosher, of Daniel and Alice, married Emma Mason, and has five children.

Annabelle E. Mosher, of Daniel and Alice, married Levi Lynch, and has three children.

Essie Mosher, of Daniel and Alice, married Douglas Thomson; no issue.

Alice Mosher, of Daniel and Alice, married Stephen Stoddard.

Frank Mosher, of Daniel and Alice, is married and living in Chicago.

Frederick Otto Mosher, of Daniel and Alice, married, and now lives in California.

Joan Mosher, of James and Hannah Sell Fish, married David Thomson, of St. John, N. B., and had five children: — Harry Ashley, Elizabeth Sell, Lewis James, Maria Mosher, and Jane Curry.

Hannah Sell Mosher, of James and H. Sell, married Capt. William Lockhart, of Avondale, and have one son, Frederick Carleton.

Henry L. Mosher, of James and Hannah Sell, married Jennie Morris, and had four children: — Ida, Hannah Sell, Maud, and Edna. Henry L. was a sea-captain, and died on board ship of small-pox, in the China Sea. His family all survive him, and are living in New York.

Ann Maria Mosher, of James and Maria Woolaver, married Richard Mounce. James Richard is their only son. They now reside in New Westminster, British Columbia.

Thomas A. Mosher, of James and Maria, married Effie E. Chambers. Their children are: — Robert Clive, Florence Annie, Effie, Joan Thomson, Ernest B., and Paul Mosher. Thomas is a smart business man, a merchant and contractor, having, in some years, built three or four vessels, George N. Knowles being the master carpenter, modelling the ships and superintending the building.

Thomas Davis Mosher, of Nicholas and Ann Davis, married Elizabeth B. Elms, of Liverpool, G.B. They have one son, Ralph, and a daughter. Thomas is a ship master, commanding one of Capt. F. Curry's ships.

Walter P. Mosher, of Nicholas and Ann, married Edith McDonald, and had two children, Howard Nicholas and Edith. His second wife was Sarah Fitch Burgess, who has no issue. He is a joiner.

Whidden Mosher, of William and Catherine Smith, married Ruby Ward, and had one daughter, Ida Catherine. His second wife was Hannah Miller, by whom he had George Whidden, Morris Stanley, Edith Jane, James Lawson, and Harry Shaw. Whidden is by trade a ship carpenter.

Morris Mosher, of William and Catherine, was also a ship-carpenter. He married Annie Allison, and had two children, Blanche and Morris. He died suddenly.

Allen Mosher, of William and Catherine, married Maggie Allison, and has one son, Clarence Fleetwood. He is a ship joiner.

I. Ulus Mosher, of Reuben and Ann Crossley, married Mary Jane Thurlow, and had Welsford, Mary Priscilla, Bessie Laurina, Arthur and Ethel.

James Aeneas Mosher, of Reuben and Ann, married Minnie H. Marsters. They have three daughters — Annie Pearl, Marion Curry, and Lenora Mabel.

Mary Elizabeth Mosher, of Reuben and Ann, married Ambrose Vannah, and had three daughters: — Alice, Bessie, and Annie.

Thomas A. Mosher, of Reuben and Ann, married Laura Malcom, and has one son, Edwin Watson.

Ramsey H. Mosher, of Reuben and Ann, married Gertrude Whidden. They live in California, and have one son.

George W. Mosher, of Reuben and Ann, married Alena McNeilly. He is a bridge builder, and resides in California.

James D. Mosher, of Capt. James and Mary Clark, married Etta McNeil. They have no issue. He is a doctor, practising in Rawdon.

Ira M. Mosher, of Capt. James, married Martha Esther James, of London. They have one daughter, Ilean Rebecca. Ira is master of the ship "Sultan," of Windsor.

Pauline Mosher, of Capt. James, married Jamieson Ball; no issue.

Matilda Mosher, of Capt. James, married Frank McInnis, carriage builder. Their children are: Frederick,. Camilla, Maggie, Leo, and Nellie.

Clarissa Mosher, of Charles and Jane Hall, married Mr. Parker, a merchant. They have one daughter, Helen Eugenia, and reside in East Boston.

Alfred Stevens Mosher, of Charles and Jane, married Rosalia Elliott, and have two children, Edgar Morton and Mabel May. Alfred is a school teacher of high grade, teaching in Kings County, N.S.

Rachel Harriet Mosher, of Charles and Jane, married Frank Rhyoners, at Maiden, Mass, December 1st, 1890.

Emeline E. Mosher, of George and Mary O. Smith, married Lewis Wier, a school teacher. Their children are: — Melville O., Ernest M., and Harry Benjamin.

Otis B. Mosher, of George and Mary O., married Mary Alice Scott, and had one son, Harry Otis. Otis B. is a house builder in Boston.

Lucilla Blanche Mosher, of George and Mary O., married Letson M. Smith, a school teacher. They have one son, Arthur Trevor.

Lydia Elvira Mosher, of George and Mary O., married J. Ambrose Brennan, 30th October, 1890. They reside at Jamaica Plains, Mass.

Brenton A. Mosher, of Noah and Ann Clark, married Annie Dodge. They have two children, Elizabeth Aldana and Frederick Aubrey.

Lydia Leila Mosher, of Noah and Ann, married Arthur J. Wier, September 24th, 1890. They reside in Newport, Hants.

Levina Mosher, of Joseph and Lucy Clark, granddaughter of Nicholas Mosher, of Walton, Hants, married Mr. O'Hara. They have three sons and one daughter, and live at East Saginaw, Michigan, U.S.

Harriet Mosher, of above Joseph, married Abel Stone. They have four boys and three girls, and reside in East Saginaw, Michigan.

Lucy Mosher, of above Joseph, married Chaunsey Cutler. They have two daughters, and also reside in East Saginaw.

The above three men work in the mills at that place.

Emma Mosher, of John and Sarah Greeno, married John Ingram. She died young, leaving no issue.

Sylvia Mosher, of John and Sarah, married Eunice Densmore, and lives in Noel. They have three daughters and one son, whose name is Stanley.

Prescott Mosher, of John and Sarah, married Priscilla Faulkner. They have four children, — Sarah, Emma, Louisa and Elvey. Prescott is light-house keeper at Burntcoat.

Ada Mosher, of John and Sarah, married Robert Densmore, and had one daughter, Georgia. She died young.

Harry Herminius Mosher, of John and Sarah, married Margaret Jannah White; they have three children, — John Clifford, Carrie, and a baby. Harry runs the sawmill at Bear Brook, East Hants.

Sarah Mosher, of William and Ann Emery, married Edmond Davis, of Port Hope, Ontario. Their children are: — Ernest W., Harold E., Charles A., and Norman F. Davis. They reside at Port Hope.

Carrie Mosher, of William and Ann, married Walter Randall, of Toronto, and had one daughter. She died when this child was nine days old.

Harriet Emma Mosher, of William and Ann, married Abner Price. Their children are: — William R. and Gordon W. They reside in Toronto.

Annie Mosher, of William and Ann, married Fred. Adams. Reuben F. Adams is their only son. They reside in Toronto.

Mary Ann Mosher, of Hiram and Eliza Emery, married William Crane. They also reside in Toronto, and have one child.

Ninth Generation

Kempt Family

Seward Mosher, of Bayard and Sarah Jane Galbraith, married Agnes Spears; their children are: Sarah Galbraith, Agnes Spears, Margaret, and Laura. Seward Mosher is a deep sea ship-master of note.

John Fulton Mosher, of Bayard and Sarah Jane, married Margaret Harvie, (of Abel). They have six children: — Edna, Robert, Ruth, Charles Bayard, Esther Jane, and William Gladstone.

Jehu Andrew, of Bayard and Sarah, married Fanny Malcom, (of Thomas), whose children are:— Frederick, Roy, Leila, Arthur, and two others, a boy and girl.

Thomas Mosher, of Bayard and Sarah, married Edith Card; no issue.

Martha Jane Mosher, of Bayard and Sarah, manned Herbert Worthy. They have one son and one daughter, and live in New Mexico, Maine, U.S.

Mary Matilda Mosher, of Bayard, married David Gleason; no issue.

Eliza Mosher, of Bayard, married John McDonald, and has two children, Johnson and Annie.

Esther Mosher, of Bayard, married William Henry Harvie. They have two sons, Harry and Seward.

George William Mosher, of Bayard, married in Portland, Me., and has one son.

James Robert, of Bayard, married Jenny Malcom, of Thomas. They have one son, George Bayard. James R. belongs to the Council of West Hants. He is a persevering young man, and a credit to his country.

Tenth Generation

Belonging To Newport

Loise Mosher, of David and Lydia Campbell, married Henry Campbell. Their children are: — Charles, William, Laura, Maggie, and a baby girl.

Nathaniel J. Mosher, of David and Lydia, married Isabella Hetler, of Maitland, Hants County. They had a daughter Isabella. The mother died when the child was eight days old. This child is now six years old, and is the eleventh generation of the Mosher family. Nathaniel Mosher is a house joiner, and works in Boston, Mass.

Philip Mosher, of Joseph, settled in St. Martins, formerly known as Quaco, N.B. He was the ancestor of both the Smith and the Black families, of Newport, also of the Cutten family, of Onslow, N.S., and the Moshers of New Brunswick are the descendants of Philip Mosher, except the emigrants from Newport.

Greeno Family

Moses Greeno and wife emigrated to this country about the time James Mosher and family came to Newport. His brother Daniel also came about this time. He married Elizabeth Wheeden, by whom he had one son, William. This son married Sarah Burgess, and had several children. He met his death in a very sudden and painful manner while attending a grist mill on Kempt Shore. In some way his coat caught in the cog wheel, and he was drawn into the wheels and instantly killed. Daniel's wife dying, he married a Miss Steel, and had eleven children: — Allen, Samuel, Moses, Major, Robert, Elizabeth, Hannah, Abigail, Sarah, Priscilla and Polly (or Mary).

Previous to the departure of Moses and Daniel from Rhode Island, the Indians were very troublesome. The Greeno brothers and others were sent by the authorities to Lake George, in the State of New York, to watch the Indians. While there in 1759, a friend of theirs, Asa Corillis, made a powder horn, upon which were engraved representations of beasts, birds, etc., together with the date, 1759, and his name. Daniel brought the horn to Nova Scotia with him. It came to Robert, and after the death of Robert and his sons it was given to the writer, as a keepsake, by Mary, Robert's widow, so I am the owner of the horn at this date, June, 1891.

Allen Greeno (of Daniel) married Jane Andress. His second wife was Mary Campbell.

Samuel Greeno married Phoebe Burgess.

Moses Greeno married Mary Bailer.

Major Greeno married Margaret Harvie.

Robert Greeno married Mary Densmore.

Elizabeth Greeno married William Tomlinson.

Hannah Greeno married Jehu Mosher.

Priscilla Greeno married Joseph Mosher.

Polly Greeno married Nicholas Mosher.

Sarah Greeno married Robert Harvie.

Abigail Greeno married William Hill.

John Anthony's Family

John Anthony married Ruth Allen, sister of James Mosher's wife. He came from Rhode Island and settled on a farm adjoining the Township of Newport line. His children were — Noah, Alice, Annie, David, James and John, and others who were left in Rhode Island. Annie married John Burgess, at the mouth of the Kennetcook River, north side, and had Mary and other children. Mary married Jehu Mosher (of Jehu). Alice married Ezekiel Marsters, of the above place. One son, Daniel, is now living. He is 87 years old. The above John Anthony died March 31st, 1808.

Shipbuilding

The first vessel built in Nova Scotia was built at Little Harbor, Kelly's Cove, Yarmouth Co., in 1764. The anchors were forged at that place by Mr. Neal, a German. The vessel registered 18 tons. Another shallop was built at Fish Point, Yarmouth Co., the same year.

The first vessel of much size (after N. Mosher built the sloop) in Newport was built at the mouth of Kennetcook River, on Card's Beach, by Job Card and sons, in 1819. Her construction was superintended by Robert Knight, of Maine, U. S. She was brig rigged; was named the "Commerce," and was sailed by the Card boys.

The first vessel built at Newport Landing (now called Avondale) was the brig "Hiram," for Capt. Sweet. Her building was superintended by master builder Hallett, of Maine. She was launched in 1826, and was lost December 24th, 1831, while coming into the bay from the West Indies. It was during a terribly cold time, and the vessel got iced up so that she was unmanageable. She went ashore at Gulliver's Hole, near Digby. Capt. Jas. Liswell was master, and Capt. Sinclair chief mate. They were both drowned, with two others, when trying to get ashore. John Liswell, a brother of the captain, and John Lockhart got ashore safely.

In April, 1845, John Liswell was master of the brig "Leone." He was said to be a smart man. His vessel was last seen beating out the South Channel while bound to New York from Windsor. The brig and all hands, eight in number, all from Newport, were never heard of again. Capt. James W. Liswell, now master of the barque "Mark Curry," is the only son of the late Capt. John Liswell.